Dedication

I dedicate this book to people who have forgotten about themselves.

Testimonial

Viv brought me back from the brink, I was existing not living, I couldn't function life was numb I was there but not there. I had no confidence. I couldn't concentrate; the lights were on but no one was home.

Through empowerment I can hear the birds sing, hear the breeze through the trees, hear my children laugh, see my wife smile, communicate my feelings without breaking down; cope with difficult situations. There's still a long way to go, but instead of giving up on life I can embrace it and be a part of it.

Thank You,

Viv

Empowerment

Forty-nine tools

Viv Zicari

Published by Vivienne Zicari

All text and photographs copyright © 2017 by Vivienne Zicari. First published in 2017.

The right of (Vivienne Zicari) to be identified as the author of this work has been asserted by her in accordance with the Copyright, Designs and Patents Act 1988.

ISBN: 978-1-5272-0904-6

CONTENTS

FOREWORD

The Book of Empowerment Tools evolved from the work I have undertaken with clients during my many years practising as a counsellor and psychotherapist. My inspiration is to help people live their lives to their full potential. They owe it to themselves. This book is about my observations made along the way, as I watched the journeys that amazing individuals have made and continue to make. Without these people this book would not have been written, it was a team effort. So thank you, you all know who you are.

CHAPTER 1: INTRODUCTION TO EMPOWERMENT

In front of you is a platform. Right now you don't know how many steps it will take to reach this platform. Maybe a lot or maybe just a few. *The forty-nine Empowerment Tools* will give you the knowledge and self-understanding you need to reach this personal platform. Once you are there, you will be in a position to view your world from 360 degrees. When you are on your platform, there will be some boxes yet to be opened, but you will be in a more positive mindset to open the remaining boxes, and to do so at your leisure.

Hello, and welcome to *forty-nine Empowerment Tools* – your Empowerment Programme. Among these pages are the tools you will need to help you understand what makes you tick. In effect, the A – Z of your life. You have a real opportunity here to explore choices you have made and to gain an understanding of the people who may have influenced you in those choices.

A client working on their empowerment journey recalled a conversation, stating to their partner. "After me you are first." This client understood that for them to go forward, they had to put them self-first.

Empowerment Tool 1: *It is okay to be me.*

This statement is ambiguous, open to more than one interpretation; it's how you view your world. There are no rules except yours. Imagine the freedom at your fingertips. You can do or be anything you wish. No more worrying about what others think about you, no more trying to please everyone, no more self-critical statements, no more self-doubt. Accept this and your belief in yourself will be absolute.

If it does not feel right for you then there is a good chance it is not. Imagine feeling totally open and uninhibited in how you view your world, how you feel about something. Just allow yourself to think independently. When you accept your past mistakes, things you have said and done, and take full responsibility for your life, then you are on your way towards empowerment.

Along the way you may experience eye-opening, thought-provoking and surprising moments. Getting there is slightly more complex. This is your world so prepare for what I hope will be an enlightening journey.

Empowerment Tool 2: *I can, I want, I will.*

Think of your life as a puzzle. Some pieces are missing and you need to go and find them. Putting yourself first is a good place to start collecting those missing pieces.

We are not interested in your peripheral world, as this is about you and what you want. Clients have commented over the years that the Empowerment Programme is plain logic, but work needs to be done first of all for you to get there.

Never mind, as you already have two tools in the bag!

When was the last time you put yourself first? Think for a moment. When was the last time you said "No" with conviction? Or "I want to do this", maybe "I do not want to do that", or "I want to have a day all to myself"?

We all, at some point in our life, get into the habit of placing ourselves on a shelf. For instance, we might have our own "look at this later" shelf or "I am not ready" shelf or maybe "I don't want to think about it" shelf.

Some of us have a "worthless" shelf.

Summary of Empowerment Tools in this Chapter

1) *It's okay to be me*

2) *I can, I want, I will*

CHAPTER 2: THE JOURNEY

Early in my practice as a counsellor and psychotherapist I noticed a recurring theme when talking to clients; they did not seem to figure at all in their own lives. This led me to sit down and have a long think. Then I noted down my findings and observations. The next step was to test this theory on myself.

I discovered to my amazement it was the Empowerment Tools that gave me back me; it is as simple as that. During my years of study, then while building my business, and in my private life, I had gotten into the habit of giving, i.e. being there for others, which I did happily and willingly. The problem that had arisen was that I had forgotten about myself along the way.

So I made the conscious decision to give myself time to reflect and ask myself important questions; for instance, was I happy for the sake of others?

Empowerment Tool 3: *Where do I figure in my life?*

Empowerment Tool 4: *Am I content with my achievements both personal and professional*?

Empowerment Tool 5: *Am I in control of my life*?

Empowerment Tool 6: *Can I make an independent decision*?

Empowerment is not about huge changes to your peripheral life, but you do need to pay attention to analysing your internal dialogue, your core, the part of yourself rarely shared. This is a main player where your decision-making is concerned.

Empowerment Tool 7: *Do I feel my relationships are 50/50?*

Are my relationships equal, that is, 50-50? Or do I occupy a higher percentage? Empowerment requires a great deal of reflection; not only self-reflection but also reflecting on the world you live in, encompassing all relationships, whether personal or professional. This carries a heavy influence on how you think, feel, and behave.

Empowerment Tool 8: *What are my dreams and goals? What am I doing or not doing correctly when I try to attain those goals? What am I missing?*

Social rules stipulate you do not think about yourself but think about others. What do you think of that and do you agree?

Maybe you have inadvertently been following social rules. If so, then it's hardly surprising if you have difficulty listing what you like and lack the self-confidence to voice your opinions. Empowerment does not burden itself with confrontation with your peripheral or social world. Rather, it encourages you to confront your internal dialogue.

You have lived with you all your life and no one knows you like you do. For example, a woman was asked for a signature from someone who knew her really well to support her passport application, so she signed it herself. When asked by her family why she had done this, she replied indignantly, "Well, nobody knows me like I do."

You really are the most important person in your life and this is why empowerment begins solely with you. Once you understand and accept this then all anxiety, endlessly worrying about things you can never change, fear of certain situations, people, and anger will disappear.

Empowerment Tool 9: *People are not my responsibility. I am responsible only for myself. I cannot change people but I can change me.*

Think for a moment about this statement: *Ninety percent of what makes you unhappy, insecure, fearful, angry, sad, stressed and anxious is not yours*.

Think about your observations of those who have influenced your life and people who are on your peripheral. Think about their worldview, their behaviour patterns, and how perhaps you have inadvertently incorporated them and made a part of your makeup. The next time you experience a negative feeling, try asking yourself – is it yours or theirs? Check in before hastily checking out or you'll allow those negative feelings to swallow you up.

Empowerment Tool 10: *Who am I? (Identity)*

I would like to share with you what I consider one very important Empowerment Tool – Identity. It was one of my lecturers who made this tool become more clear to me. I recall one afternoon we were seated in our usual semicircle, when he said, "I am going to ask you a question and I would like you to answer spontaneously."

We all nodded in earnest.

"Who are you?" he asked.

After a moment's hesitation, we began: *I am a mother, I am a father; a sister, brother.* Some people gave their profession, etc. You get the idea. The lecturer was very patient as the group was quite large, but he listened attentively until we were done. He then stood up and walked behind his desk without saying a word. He looked briefly at his notes then looked up at us.

"Thank you," he smiled, "but you have not answered my question." You could have heard a pin drop. "No," he said, "*I asked, who are you? Not what you are.*"

Summary of Empowerment Tools in this Chapter

3) *Where do I figure in my life?*

4) *Am I content with my achievements, both personal and professional?*

5) *Am I in control of my life?*

6) *Can I make an independent decision?*

7) *Do I feel my relationships are 50/50?*

8) *What are my dreams and goals? What am I doing or not doing correctly when I try to attain those goals? What am I missing?*

9) *People are not my responsibility. I am only responsible for myself. I cannot change people, but I can change myself.*

10) *Who am I? (Identity)*

CHAPTER 3: GROUP IDENTITY

Following on from Empowerment Tool 10, "Who am I", let's think about identity in a little more detail. All too often we use identity to define who we think we are. In fact, identity is how social rules and people identify and judge us; it has nothing to do with our individuality. Empowerment is all about individuality and autonomy.

In the first or second session, I usually ask my client to imagine a group in any setting and then say where they would choose to sit – at the front, middle, back or on the aisle.

The point of this exercise is to develop a powerful sense of self-observation by using a group scenario, where the individual identifies themselves within social rules of communication both verbal and behavioural, to define personality types.

I would like you to think back to your time at school. Looking at group structures, where do you think you would place yourself? Did you lead, or were you happier just to conform and go along with the majority? Were you the one caring for others in a group? Were you a part of a few groups? Did you like to flit in and out?

Groups can be large or small. You might have belonged to many groups, or to one small group of perhaps two or three. But the same question applies – where do you think you fitted in?

Empowerment Tool 11: *Social groups, where do I fit in*?

Imagine rows of chairs in a hall. You can sit anywhere you choose, but do not concern yourself with why you are there, as this would depend on the situation. Just go with your instincts.

Now picture a hall filled with chairs and imagine yourself. Where would you instinctively sit? Maybe you'd stand? In the front row or around the front, in the middle, perhaps towards the back and preferably behind a pillar? Is it important to have your back against a wall? Perhaps you would choose to sit on the aisle, either towards the front, in the middle, or at the back of the hall?

I use the following for my own personal guide, built on the observations accrued through my work over the years with clients.

The Front

Those who choose the front middle have a tendency towards the alpha/leader mentality, are highly competitive and in most cases dominant – not necessarily through choice but through learnt behaviour – and this is how within social rules, they define their identity. From a nurturing perspective think of Boudicca staff in hand follow me I will lead the way. The problem which arises from this philosophy going forward is fine, but what is happening behind you or to the side, how much is the Boudicca in you missing? This is your survival strategy, existing but not permitting yourself to live your life to your full potential.

From a business perspective, this group often, but not always, maintain narcissistic traits, are self-consumed into adulthood. Their need to prove themselves to the point of exhaustion often develops into obsessional behaviour. It is important, even vital, to their survival to be noticed. They have a get-things-done attitude. They are usually perfectionists, and expect others around them to deliver no less than one hundred percent.

People front middle are hooked on adrenaline, they are risk takers and love the buzz it gives them to win that contract, to go beyond being just average. Above all they need to stand out in a crowd. They rarely have limits as they see their life and opportunities as limitless. Their outlook on life leans towards the objective as opposed to the subjective. They have little time for tantrums, unless they are the person having one, in which case they believe they are totally justified.

At school they excelled, not always academically, but certainly socially. They are experts on reading people. That expertise is a natural gift and gives them a deep-seated sense of belief in whatever they do. They further believe they will always succeed and they are absolute masters when it comes to manipulating others. They are notable for being great charmers and have the ability to manage people effectively. They make things happen and are prepared to go to any lengths and make any sacrifice to get the result they desire.

All these things they consider to be key strategies needed to succeed. Not all front-centre personalities have completed higher education; they will nevertheless have travelled through the ranks with breath-taking speed and they do not like to fail. They seek the necessary know-how to ensure they reach their goals. These attributes make them highly attractive to an employer, although their natural preference is to be self-employed and their employers serve only as stepping stone towards their ultimate quest or goal.

The downside of this type of personality from a nurture and business perspective, is the pressure with which they burden themselves. They can be fraught with problems from perhaps having grown up in an alpha household.

Imagine the heavy burden the alpha sets himself up for; a down day, not tolerated, *I can and will succeed, onwards, and upwards.*

This personality has a plethora of mottos. Whether they truly believe what they are saying is another matter, as fear drives them. Fear of losing it all, loss of control, fear of failure, fear of abandonment, fear of losing the respect of others, fear of losing their place in society; a king will never willingly give up his crown, he will fight to the bitter end, this is the leader's mindset.

While the rest of us can change career, lifestyle, and attitude – these changes naturally occur as we progress through our life – the front-middle personality's mindset is locked firmly into the idea that "the world is mine to conquer", often only to find it's dominion reduced over the years to a virtual crawl space.

As most people get older it's not as important, but the front-middle personality enjoys the buzz, rarely misses an opportunity, though oddly enough they are only ever in competition with themselves. Failure is not in their remit and the natural progression of time brings a strain; where once they could meet challenges, they can never now admit the struggle to succeed is all a bit too much. This would be perceived by themselves as failure.

Stimulants such as drugs and alcohol are prevalent in this group. Interestingly, this seems to be the one area that the front-middle person cannot control. Front-middle personalities liken drugs and alcohol to the addictive buzz, the adrenaline rush they experience when pursuing a new challenge. Depression is a common theme presented in therapy by front-middle personalities, becoming a problem when they realise that, for whatever reason, they can no longer live their lives in the fast lane. The survival of those with such a personality hinges on success, in how they perceive their identity within society and within social rules.

The Middle

Moving onto the middle group personality, safety in numbers comes to mind. Members of this group do not want to take the lead, but have learnt to follow social rules. These rules are to smile, appear happy, be enthusiastic, and above all survive.

You can see this person at school, in a group, following the leader, ever watchful, aware, never relaxing. They feel as if they are adrift on a boat in a vast ocean with no oars, and at the mercy of wherever the current chooses to take them. They perceive every possibility as a danger and live their lives in flight mode. They have witnessed the swift brutality of the group mindset towards other members, and so the middle personality does not enjoy being challenged; this would make them visible and this personality does not want to stand out no matter the cost.

Survival begins at birth; the infant is born to survive from the moment it takes its first breath. The caregiver, whether biological or non-biological, denotes life or death for the child, regardless how they treat the child. Even when ridiculed and rejected, the child will return repeatedly. This is our most basic and primal need; no logic, objectivity or subjectivity play a role here. It is survival of the fittest.

The person who chooses the middle of the group subconsciously understands the rules of survival. For whatever reason their personal history indicates, they do not feel strong enough to take the lead. They want to be an integral part of the group so as to remain safe. So they adopt a passive/submissive role, one often tried-and-tested, observed from home life.

If you have identified yourself in this group, I would like you to think of the perceptions you had regarding other people. For instance, that they are more capable than you, that no-one is as shy as you, that no one lacks confidence as you do. You may also think they are more intelligent or witty than you, better looking than you. Middle personalities are masters at making presumptions, even though their only route they have taken to this presumption is an extension of their worldview.

The downside to the middle personality is that there is little or no personal growth. These people often become listeners not by choice but from the necessity to belong. They are chameleons ready to adapt to any situation as it arises; become an agony aunt, carer, ally. They are people pleasers and will do almost anything for anybody. They are also the most put upon and most likely to experience abuse, as they find it difficult to say no out of fear of rejection or being ostracised by their group.

They suppress thoughts and hurtful experiences that add up significantly over the years. Moreover, they often lament the fact that their friends never listen to them or help them when they need help, but equally they find it very difficult to share their true feelings out of fear of ridicule, rejection or being misunderstood.

This personality does not like to stand out where decision making is concerned. They take their time, are always hesitant, do nothing impulsive, give careful consideration, play it safe, and nearly always follow the lead, regardless whether they agree with the decision or not, which only adds to their sense of worthlessness.

The Back

To understand the personality type at the back of the group consider a shepherd, or shepherdess; before them is their flock, they are life's nurturers, constantly on the lookout for someone who might need their help. This personality's survival is all about doing for others and the feel-good factor it brings to them. The need to be needed, their very existence depends on who, or how many, people need or depend on them.

The shepherds are in some form like that of being a parent or carer, as this really is their life long ticket towards nurturing. However, the back of the group personality subconsciously uses this nurturing aspect of themselves as a way to belong, as they lack the self-confidence to step forward and take control of their life. In this way they live through others.

Similarly, to the middle group personality, the survival of this personality depends on need, and their identity is heavily involved with social rules – how society looks upon the group – as vital to its very core.

Where else would we find our volunteers, the good Samaritans, carers of humans and animals? This group is genuine, extremely loyal, and more likely than any other personality type to take charge if they feel their flock is under threat. The shepherd is very generous, if not over generous to the point of self-sacrifice, giving support to whoever needs their help.

However, while this group has only the best of intentions, they can inadvertently smother other individual's natural growth, and they can find it very difficult to let go, because this would place the focus on them, and their whole existence is about deflection.

This personality type is so passionate and sincere in what they do for others, and their empathy is projected towards whatever cause they are currently supporting. They do not seek stardom but in their own way seek to do what they feel is right. However, in equal measure they take little time in getting to know who they are, or meet their needs.

Survival for members in this group is solely dependent on other people's need for them. I truly admire this group as they will go all out to defend and fight the cause of those they identify as vulnerable, but I equally wonder who is truly vulnerable here?

Although this group's survival is dependent on belonging or being needed, their identity is embedded in social rules. They often speak through others, or a cause, because deep down they lack self-confidence, and self-belief.

The shepherd/shepherdess is all about self-sacrifice, while quietly praising themselves that they were of some help. If you take away everything upon which their survival and identity hinges, what does this group have left? What does a shepherd do without his flock?

The Aisle

The aisle personality desperately wants to be a part of the particular group they are sitting on the edge of, either front, middle or back, but they seek an escape route. Escaping situations appears to be inherent in their behaviour patterns. They err on the side of caution while craving to be a part of a group.

This group has a remarkable in-built hypersensitive antenna tuned to rejection, their personal trigger.

Imagine a group of friends at school, let's say during lunchbreak. There is a bench free but it only sits three people and there are four in the group. The alpha (self-appointed leader) will naturally occupy a seat on the bench. The other two seats could be occupied by a middle personality, willing to please, and a shepherd anxious to take care of the group. The remaining person – who does not get a seat – is usually an aisle personality.

This personality would not feel comfortable being so close to the group; their survival technique is to either use humour or to play the victim. They know flavour of the month is prevalent in groups, and they need to analyse the mood of the group so as to determine which role they will currently play.

The aisle personality feels they do not fit in, and goes through life in that way well into adulthood. They are the observers of the group. Their goal is to belong, and they are aware that their position in the group is only as good as their last performance – hence the quick exit strategy.

This personality generally lacks feelings of self-worth, they find it difficult to trust and to reveal their feelings, possibly out of fear of ridicule, and rejection; they can only be their true selves when they are alone. Like the middle personality, they are prone to depression. They are often exhausted playing various roles dependent upon who they are with, and at some point in their lives they realise the depth of their loneliness, which often results in prolonged periods of depression.

These people have what I term a very strong core, meaning they possess a deep-down resolve, which, when tapped into, digested, understood, and accepted, demonstrates that their capabilities know no bounds.

They are already experts in observation. If they put as much effort into listening to themselves and worked on achieving their goals, instead of devoting energy on fitting into various roles, these marvellous individuals could do so much more with their lives.

This personality type's ultimate goal is to belong. Choices they make invariably reflect where they want to be seen within social groups. Similarly, to the middle personality, they do not challenge – usually out of fear of rejection.

Conclusion

I hope you are beginning to understand how complex we are? Perhaps you might identify yourself in various roles in the group, dependent upon your life situations? Perhaps you can identify with a part of one group but also find yourself adding your own thoughts, which is great.

Listen to what you have to say, what you think is relevant to you. This is what empowerment is all about; it is about *you*, just you, no one else. Guard against critical self-statements as they serve no purpose other than make you feel useless and worthless.

Empowerment does not take away a person's identity, but it does challenge the perception the individual has about their identity, and why a person has chosen to sit in a particular group.

So what is the point? Awareness is the key, together with evaluating whether you are content to play these various roles, or whether you find them a strain. Just being aware is an amazingly positive sign as you are concentrating on you and that your subconscious is beginning to awaken.

Go ahead, challenge what I have to say. Disagree with me, consider your own worldview and your opinions. This book is about *you* and your journey. If you ignore what I have to say, then ask yourself why. You really do have all the answers. Go find them.

Summary of Empowerment Tools in this Chapter

11) *Social groups, where do I fit in?*

CHAPTER 4: EMPOWERED YOU BEGINS TO EMERGE

In the first three chapters we explored identity and survival in how we interact within social rules and with each other.

I hope now you are examining your memories and that you are connecting the dots of your life. I hope too you are beginning to find those missing puzzle pieces.

Most of the memories will be negative, as we are genetically wired to recall negatives as opposed to positives. I explain to clients how negatives have played a vital role in human evolution. For example, when our species was evolving we lived a highly primitive existence but we instinctively understood the rules of survival. If we skipped out of our dwelling admiring the sun, trees, flowers, and ignored a large carnivore stalking us, we would not have survived as a species. If, however, we left our dwelling with caution and looked upon our world with a negative and mistrustful mindset, we would be aware of danger but above all we would have done everything in our power to survive.

Today, we may no longer consider ourselves primitive but we continue to practise caution. Do you recall those instructions you were given as a teenager just before you went out with friends for an evening?

Be careful, never trust anyone, look out for danger, be on your guard – err on the side of caution. We are both genetically and socially geared towards negativity and survival.

This part of the programme can be the most challenging and intensive, but it is also where the most positive shifts generally begin to take shape. From this point the client progressively takes on the leadership role in their life.

Empowerment Tool 12: You are entitled to your views.

Introducing the all-important worldview, how you view your world, and interpret your world through your experiences. After all, they are based on your own observations. So I ask the obvious question: What is wrong with that? People are entitled to disagree with you as they too have their world view.

The outcome of any debate depends largely upon acquired behaviour and life influences. Would you describe yourself as passive? Are you easily swayed in a discussion? Are you filled with self-doubt and lack self-belief? Do you have difficulty in trusting what you say and often feel guilty?

For example, would you agree that, "I don't like confrontation; I think of an answer later which I would have liked to have said, but people always seem to twist the conversation. So I give in or feel guilty if I do not agree."

Perhaps you would describe yourself as authoritative. Do you feel you are always right? Maybe you feel you must have the last word in any discussion and will wear someone down until they agree with you. For example, "I have a rule of thumb, my way of thinking is the right way, it has served me well in my life and I see no reason why I should change the way I think."

Once you incorporate empowerment into your life, you will no longer have a problem with passivity or authoritativeness, because neither will be relevant to you. Your attitude will become "I will not be ruled by another and I understand everyone has their point of view."

Imagine all that energy expended and taking on someone's negativity when there really is no need; just being you is all it takes – other people are not your responsibility. If you feel the need to jump in and save someone, stop for a moment and ask yourself who you're really trying to save.

Empowerment Tool 13: *Do I try to save people*?

If you find yourself disagreeing with what I am writing, then ask yourself why? What have you read that has evoked an emotion or a memory? Explore more closely what you are thinking and feeling. Don't fob yourself off with your usual rhetoric. You owe it to yourself to be honest, no more hiding.

If you want to change your life then you need to start asking pertinent questions and challenging your responses. That is what I am doing here; challenging you to think independently. Taking control of your life is to begin doing things you don't feel comfortable doing but pushing yourself to do them anyway. Once you are able to cast doubts aside and stop making excuses there is no limit to what you can achieve. You will have self-belief. This is the point at which my clients usually talk about their 'eureka moments'.

I have spoken at length about society and how we interact with others from the moment we're born. But we also learn through others; for instance, the do's and don'ts, rights, and wrongs. From an educational perspective, society's expectations are for us to interact, be supportive towards each other, do well with our studies and to be confident in our abilities; these will enhance our career prospects and so make us a valuable member of society.

It sounds really good on paper, doesn't it? But here I am some seventeen years later practising as a therapist and I'm still waiting to meet the person who has fulfilled all of society's criteria. I believe these unfulfilled criteria are why negativity is inherent within us. That the emphasis on negativity is not only genetic, but that it is continually re-enforced within society. Effectively, we are from birth programmed to fail.

Consider this conundrum from your ever growing empowerment perspective. Interaction and supporting others is absolutely fine, but where do you think you figure within this statement? As a hint, remember the group analogy; where would you place yourself in the group in terms of interaction, and support? Just let your thoughts wander, do not try to find answers, let them come naturally. Trust yourself. You really do have all the answers.

Empowerment Tool 14: *What are my perceptions of what others think about me?*

Doing well in our studies can be a huge part of our being accepted. How academic or non-academic we believe others to perceive us to be can strongly influence our personal relationships.

Children look for appraisal as this denotes survival, fitting in and acceptance, so we need to get it right. The child returns home with a grade A and is usually applauded. The child's internal dialogue is perhaps "Okay I need to keep this up, I must get it right, I want everyone to be proud of me, I like the attention."

Such is an introduction to a probable life of placing themselves under stress, thinking they must always achieve, fearing failure, non-acceptance and personal anger if they do not get it right every time.

Perhaps the child returns home with a D or E. What will the probable reaction be? The child is told to work harder and their internal dialogue is "I didn't please them, I failed."

Introduction to a lifelong feeling of anxiety associated with getting things wrong leads to self-confidence taking a nosedive, which in turn leads to fear of failure, non-acceptance, and anger that the child has failed in the eyes of their caregivers.

Or perhaps you grew up in a household where any grade was treated with indifference? In that case the child's inner dialogue becomes "I am not good enough, I am a failure, no one cares." This is an introduction to a life dominated by a lack of self-confidence, self-worth, anger, rejection, stress, all stemming from a failure to please.

These are just a few examples, but these experiences can so easily leave a child with a template of education so that any future learning or trying anything new is linked with fear of failure, which is carried long into adulthood. You subconsciously place this bad experience and associated feelings into numerous other scenarios you experience along the way. It all starts with one bad experience, one bad memory, one bad feeling. If you need to go over this passage a couple of times then do so. It is important that you understand that early experiences and memories linked to those experiences really can have a lifelong impact on you. Please remember you are not looking to blame anyone here. This is about you putting to bed any negative feelings. Just keep asking yourself "What is relevant today compared with what I experienced as a child?"

Society expects us to be confident in our abilities, as this will enhance our career prospects. We have already run the gauntlet and most of us have experienced success and failure in some way. At either end of the spectrum I would say confidence is frail at the best of times. Lack of confidence is often linked to not feeling safe, attempting to try or being forced to do something despite it being unfamiliar, just to fit in. It is time to have a chat with yourself when a challenge arises and you automatically take a step back, ask yourself why? What is it that is stopping you from going forward. If each answer you give yourself is negative, then challenge that negative thought. It is perfectly normal to get annoyed when challenged, as this is your protective mode. Dig deeper into your fears as the answer is there – go find it.

I always say to clients as we begin working together that they really do know all the answers, but that circumstances, personal history, learnt behaviour, historic influences, have all played a part in blurring that path. Other influences are what they feel they should say, their conscious mind being in the moment, and what they truly feel but are afraid to say for whatever personal reasons their sub-conscious mind. For example: "I am known as the happy guy, I make people laugh, I have loads of friends, I play different roles depending on who I am with. Who would want to know the real me?"

Empowerment Tool 15: *What triggers my anger*?

During the sessions, I often ask clients what their interpretation is regarding emotions. I notice that clients are quite content to talk about various emotions but talking about anger is rarely forthcoming. Anger is a relevant emotion. It is okay to feel angry, to understand when you are angry and to tell someone you are feeling angry and why. So I would like you the reader to think about your personal anger triggers. What makes you angry, why do you get angry?

It is very difficult to self-analyse when all you have is your own worldview. When you find yourself going around in circles and never finding the answer you are looking for? It's so frustrating. The empowerment tools are here to encourage you to move beyond your worldview, to take a look at yourself and your influences from a different perspective or angle; to observe where you would place yourself in the group structure. This is where observation, both internal and external, becomes effective.

A person doesn't just arrive at a particular age realising they have issues which have impacted or currently impact on their lives, as this has usually been a long haul and often an exhausting process. For example, you may have shared your concerns with family members or close friends, but in doing so you were attempting to take advice from people who are only capable of seeing the problem presented from their worldview. They will usually give examples of similar situations, which sound perfectly logical from *their* perspective but as this is their own worldview, can they realistically come up with an answer with which you can totally identify and act upon?

Summary of Empowerment Tools in This Chapter

12) *You are entitled to your views because they are based on your*

   observations.

13) *Do I try to save people?*

14) *What are my perceptions of what others think about me?*

15) *What triggers my anger?*

CHAPTER 5: CHILDHOOD

Your instinctive need is to survive, to fit into society and for society to accept you. Being alone leaves you feeling vulnerable and you need to feel you belong. So where does this all begin for us? Let us take a look at childhood.

What I am about to write in no way points a finger at your main caregivers, whether biological or non-biological. This is important. You have your worldview, and they have their worldview, no matter how close a relationship you may enjoy or have enjoyed with your main caregivers. Please remember we are concentrating on your individuality, your perspective, your worldview.

The journey from the cradle to adulthood is not an easy one. From the moment of birth, you began the learning process and took on influences along the way. These remain with you but here is your opportunity: you can determine if those influences are helpful and if you should continue to incorporate them into your life. What you do with them is always your choice.

Start with a blank page: What would you put on that first page? Well, your main caregiver is usually the safest bet because this is where your most basic needs were being met; protection, safety and survival at the stage when you were at your most vulnerable and needy.

Although there might be other family members around, the main caregiver and food bearer is the one to watch until you learn to communicate and broaden your world. This first attachment appears to be, historically, the strongest bond. Unconditional love or indifference might develop into a positive or negative relationship as the years go by. This first bonding enabled you to survive. Without it you would not be here, love it or hate it, but do not underestimate the power of this first experience, which appears to endure for a lifetime.

Guilt, criticism, abandonment, mistrust, deceit, rejection, overprotection and anger often reside within this first bonding, for many who have not experienced a good relationship with their main caregivers and continue to carry these negative memories well into adulthood. I have lost count of the times clients have said in a matter of fact tone "My main caregiver or caregivers did not listen to me, so why would anyone else be interested in what I have to say?" Or "He/she thought I was useless so it must be true" or perhaps "He/she told me I was ugly, and no one will ever want me." Maybe "My mother offers unconditional love, something my husband cannot seem to do."

I wonder why memories, words or actions carry such an impact on us well into adulthood? Do you still see caregivers as a type of life support? If you disagree with them or stand your ground, do you believe you will not be able to survive without them? Why do we automatically incorporate childhood memories and feelings into our adult world even though they do not logically have a place? A good way to make sense of this negativity is to think about the caregiver in more detail, take a look at their upbringing, go as far back as you can and ask yourself "What made him or her so bitter, unhappy, angry, insecure? What happened to them during their childhood?"

Rather than looking at your main caregiver or caregivers from a negative perspective, try your hand as a detective. You can remain as angry and hurt as you choose. Although you may never forgive your caregivers, perhaps if you gain some knowledge as to why they treated you a certain way, you may over time understand that it was never anything to do with you, but somehow you were simply unfortunate. You were innocently caught up in the firing line of an adult venting their unhappiness, insecurities and learnt behaviour patterns.

Another subconscious element crucial to the child's learning is the art of mimicking through observation. The infant will often take on the characteristics of its main caregiver, mimicking their facial expressions and body language in an attempt to feed itself. Eventually, the child comprehends words. Using mimicry, the child will negate its way through this maze long before it realises which are the right words, and in what context they are used. The one thing the child does understand from an early age is how to prompt a response. The reactions of the child's main caregivers, whether positive or negative, give the child the crucial tools with which they will conduct themselves in society when they reach adulthood.

Mimicry is a way we subconsciously connect, a basic but extremely effective form of communication. This comes in handy when attempting to fit in, to be a part of, or seeking acceptance. These things are all heavily involved in the subconscious art of mimicking. Typical forms of mimicking are dressing in a similar way, agreeing readily with someone, liking the same things, copying how someone speaks, their mannerisms, and behaviour. All these techniques are learnt subconsciously from childhood. They might make a person feel as though they 'belong', but the question "Who am I?" remains when you think about your main caregivers.

Empowerment Tool 16: *Can I identify with my caregivers' passive or authoritative traits?*

Empowerment Tool 17: *How would I describe myself, passive or authoritative?*

Empowerment Tool 18: *Which caregiver am I more like in terms of my character?*

Empowerment Tool 19: *Which caregiver am I more like in terms of my behaviour?*

My clients have often associated themselves with one caregiver, but equally identify other traits of their character or behaviour with another caregiver. Just being aware is the key. You might discover that you have inadvertently adopted a behaviour pattern which was never yours in the first place.

How do you feel today when you think about these memories? Just allow yourself to be honest with yourself. No one needs to know these thoughts. They are private and no one else's business. There are no negatives here. All we are doing is slowly opening the door to your awareness. What you do with it is your choice. Hold onto it for the time being and build upon it as more revelations begin to appear. Or act upon it. Either way the awareness is yours and you may do with it as you wish.

Perhaps it is time to clear out your emotional chest of draws, one drawer at a time. Courage is required to open the first drawer and take a look at your life. Remember, ninety percent of what you carry is in all likelihood not even yours. Try not to get caught up in blaming others. It really is a complete waste of your time and energy. Identify the cause, give yourself time to adjust, go over the scenarios in your mind as often as you need to, until you can finally say to yourself "This is not mine." Then let it go.

Remember your negative memories and feelings linked to others were never yours to begin with. They were theirs. If you have given yourself time to think about your main caregivers and their histories, and reached an understanding as to why they were the way they were, congratulations. It is now your choice whether you continue to carry those negative memories and feelings, or to let them go.

Empowerment Tool 20: *How relevant is the child in me today in conjunction with my caregivers and their influence?*

Empowerment Tool 21: *Have I made choices about which I didn't need advice but felt I should or must inform a relevant other?*

Empowerment Tool 22: *Have I carried a plan through to completion without anyone else's input?*

Empowerment Tool 23: *How much do I depend on my caregivers or significant others?*

Empowerment Tool 24: *Do I feel guilty if I do not do what someone has asked me to do?*

If by this stage you are beginning to allow past incidents, conversations you had, words you overheard, come through to your conscious mind, and as a result you find you are looking at one or more of your caregivers in a negative light and that this evokes anger, let that anger remain with you for a while. Anger is a strong emotion, don't dismiss it, let it run its course in your mind, and see if you can identify other emotions connected to feeling angry. If it helps, make a note of your feelings. If you do have negative feelings about your caregivers and this make you feel guilty, let us stop for a moment and look at guilt.

Empowerment sees guilt as a form of bullying in which others impose their will upon you. And yes, guilt is a learnt behaviour pattern. So the question to ask yourself is "Is this mine or theirs?"

For example: "If you don't do as I ask, then I will be disappointed in you" or "That's okay, I was hoping you could make it today but don't worry, I will cope." Equally, guilt can be a nuance, a subtle look or gesture.

Take a moment now to think about your own personal collection of guilt triggers. I would like you to take a look at this conundrum, placing yourself front and centre from an empowered perspective. Imagine you have figured out your main caregivers or those that held the greater influence in your life and put to bed your issues that arose from those relationships. You have allowed the feelings to emerge repeatedly until you have familiarised yourself to the point that you can let it go. You no longer feel under threat, obliged to obey, obliged to say yes when you really want to say no. You have taken the time to understand the diverse worldviews and learnt behaviour with which you lived. You have given due respect to each person as you fully accept they are entitled to their opinions. The difference now is that their opinions no longer impact you because they are not yours. Your internal dialogue might challenge why anyone feels they have a 'right' to put someone under pressure. I say 'right' because so often caregivers live with the mistaken belief they own their children and in turn their children owe them in some way.

I am focusing mainly on caregivers, but these ideas apply equally to people you know in general. If you feel someone has or is making you feel guilty, ask yourself why you are allowing them to have a hold over you.

Summary of Empowerment Tools in This Chapter

16) *Can I identify with my caregiver's passive or strong or authoritative traits?*

17) *How would I describe myself, passive or authoritative?*

18) *Which caregiver am I more like in terms of my character?*

19) *Which caregiver am I more like in terms of my behaviour?*

20) *How relevant is the child in me today in conjunction with my caregivers and their influence?*

21) *Have I made choices about which I didn't need advice, but felt I should or must inform a relevant other?*

22) Have I carried a plan through to completion without asking for anyone else's input?

23) How much do I depend on my caregivers or significant others?

24) Do I feel guilty if I do not do what someone has asked me to do?

CHAPTER 6: RISK AND NEGATIVE THINKING

I frequently take my clients up Mount Kilimanjaro and push them off – figuratively speaking, of course. I am introducing risk into their world – perhaps it is time for you to start that climb.

Whenever you are faced with the unknown, the knee jerk reaction is often to retreat to a place, your comfort zone, that serves no benefit. It's a place where the 'better the devil you know' philosophy prevails. If you are to progress further you need to justify that retreat to yourself.

I often say to clients that your mind is either your best friend or your worst enemy. It can help you soar to great heights and achieve the most unbelievable things, or it can reduce you to a pulp. It can keep you a virtual prisoner whilst filling you with doubts; it tells you that to stay where you are is safe. Your mind creates a comfort zone and is over-generous when telling you what you cannot do.

Let us look at some examples as a way of understanding how you put yourself in your comfort zone through the practice of negative thinking. There is a part of you that wants to make a change to your life but fear of the unknown is preventing you from reaching your goal. Chances are your fears are the echoes of experiences and memories; because it (whatever 'it' is) has happened once, it will of course happen again. Right? As negativity begins to take hold your thought processes go into overdrive, conjuring up every negative they can, trying to justify why you cannot go forward.

Empowerment Tool 25: *Do I feed myself negative thoughts*?

Now, imagine you have a cauldron that sits in the centre of your conscious mind, you need fuel to heat it up. To your left is the challenge you are attempting to sabotage, and on your right is a conveyer belt that reaches down into your subconscious mind, the place where the bad memories and negativity are usually stored. You need to justify why you cannot face the challenge, whatever it may be. You need the right amount of fuel to create an effective sabotage effect. Let's crank up the conveyer belt to your subconscious and see what it comes up with.

Here are some possible examples:

Insecurities: a tried and tested fuel which is guaranteed to halt you in your decision making.

......Into the pot

Fear of failure: no negative thinking would be complete without this little gem.

Anger: plenty of fuel here guaranteed to get the cauldron boiling, and the more historic memories and feelings that emerge, the stronger the effect.

.... Into the pot

Hurt: this burns deep, and is so easily justifiable when in negative mode.

.... Into the pot

Injustice: where would negativity be without injustice?

.... Into the pot

Betrayal: another little gem, so closely linked with hurt and anger so not to be missed out.

.... Into the pot

Anxiety: fear of failure, anger, hurt, injustice, and betrayal; you might think these are enough on their own, but they have now evoked anxiety.

Resentment: a very negative and dark fuel which brings so many memories with it, all of them usually unresolved.

…………… Into the pot

Jealousy: one of the supreme fuels, guaranteed to knock out any objective thinking; it is obsessive, time consuming, and makes you feel worthless, so is ideal for the cauldron.

…………. Into the pot

Do you reckon these will do it to get the pot boiling? If you wish to add more to the pot, then go ahead.

Okay, so now you have one or several of these feelings bubbling up inside you. Clients have noted when they bring out their personal cauldron, it really is quite addictive once they begin exploring what comes up on their conveyor belt of negative thinking. The mind is by now fully overloaded. Effectively, it shuts down and goes into protective mode and as a general rule, one of two things tend to happen – you become introverted, or go on the defensive.

Now have a long think about those feelings you directly connect with, considering what each feeling evokes in you. This part of empowerment is very personal. If you become overwhelmed then put this book down, stop, take a break and only continue when you feel you are ready.

If you feel ready to continue, let's move on.

It is not a good idea to explore too many feelings on at once, so choose one or two feelings, and work your way through them. As an example, let's look at insecurities. I do not speak for the world population here – it's impossible given everyone has their own worldview – but here are a few general points to help you get started.

Empowerment Tool 26: *Why do I feel insecure today*?

Make a mental note of the first thing or things which pop in your mind. They may not make any sense but don't worry as they eventually will.

Empowerment Tool 27: *What is my earliest memory of feeling insecure*?

The memory could be hazy but the feeling will be familiar. Think about times in your life, both personal and professional, when you have experienced similar feelings.

Empowerment Tool 28: *Is there a connection between feeling insecure and my childhood?*

There is usually a pattern and you need to go find it. Think back to your caregivers, who may have exhibited moments of insecurity. Try not to look for specifics and try not to compartmentalise. This is about your memories, your observations, and your feelings attached to those observations. For example, "Mother always felt insecure in the dark and so do I." Is this a learnt behaviour? One born out of observation and mimicry?

So now you have connected two views of the possible origins of your insecurities; one is the original experience, whilst the other is an observation of recurring episodes throughout your life.

Try to recall the feeling connected to the experience which led to you feeling insecure and let it surface for a moment. Experience is not the relevant factor here. It really does come down to our memories and the feelings evoked from those memories. This is the key. Feelings.

Now put it all together. For example, a challenge today evokes a strong feeling of insecurity in the echoes of your memories. You connect with a similar feeling in your past.

Empowerment Tool 29: *I was not born feeling insecure so how I react is likely to be based on my learnt behaviour and mimicry.*

Empowerment Tool 30: *In what way does an experience or observation as a child or adolescent have a connection with me today?*

When you have digested and made sense of your world and what this means for you, then put it into perspective and go back to your current situation. Ask yourself "Why am I feeling insecure?"

Each one of us has personal experiences and those feelings of insecurity are entwined within some of those experiences. Some you can reach fairly quickly, while others are deeply embedded, and really do affect us long into adulthood. So please give yourself time.

This chapter concentrated on risk. The risk involved you delving into your world, connecting your dots along the way. It has been a very private exploration and I hope you have been honest with yourself and continue to be honest. Your subconscious is stirring and questions will begin flowing to the conscious level of your mind. You have begun your climb, so well done. How far you climb is up to you.

Summary of Empowerment Tools in this Chapter

25) *Do I feed myself negative thoughts?*

26) *Why do I feel insecure today?*

27) *What is my earliest memory of feeling insecure?*

28) *Is there a connection between feeling insecure and my childhood?*

29) *I was not born feeling insecure so how I react is likely based on my learnt behaviour and mimicry.*

30) *In what way does an experience or observation as a child or adolescent have a connection with me today?*

In Chapter Three I spoke about group identity and personality types we assume in society. It is time to expand on this theme and for you to get a clearer idea about your personal makeup. Think about people with whom you socialise; privately, at work, school, college or university. In effect, all aspects of your life which require communication.

Empowerment Tool 31: *Am I the same person when I interact with people compared to the person I am when alone?*

I would expect a resounding no, of course not! My question to you is "Why not?" Why are you any different? You really are the same person wherever you spend your day and with whomever. The only difference is in defining between your Professional and Personal Selves, so there is no room here for different personality types, no taking the lead, fitting in, or seeking comfort. Just being you is all it takes.

Empowerment Tool 32: *To just be me, no matter where I am.*

I don't have to be somebody different to be important. I am important to me in my own right, and that is all that matters — how I feel about me.

The following are examples of the more common roles we play subconsciously in society. These are not written rules, just observations.

You are going to a job interview. You may be relaxed at home wearing comfortable clothing. Perhaps laying on the sofa, maybe listening to a family member speaking, though not necessarily with full attention. You might identify this role as belonging to your Personal Self, when you are at your most relaxed. You are in your safe zone.

Now switch to the interview. I assume you would be smartly dressed, sitting upright in your chair, and listening attentively. I assume also you are not feeling particularly comfortable. Of course, you will not turn up to an interview inappropriately dressed and allow your gaze to wander when being addressed. Interviews are many people's single biggest dread. It is where you must sell yourself if you want the job. Self-doubt is at its peak because the outcome is unknown. This feeds into your fears, and you are in your risk zone; discomfort is at its maximum. There are many emotions present, which could lead to negative thinking, but just before you start to put your cauldron on the boil, stop for a moment and ask yourself...

Empowerment Tool 33: *During an interview what role you are playing*?

Take a moment to walk yourself through this scenario. You want to show your interviewer that you are taking the potential role seriously. You dress appropriately as this is your professional self, and so there's just one role to remember. You listen attentively to what the interviewer has to say about the position. You want to know what is on offer and if this will fit with your life.

Now realise that you are in control; you cannot control the outcome of the interview but you can control your approach, execution, and proactive self-evaluation. This is your Professional Self. In this professional role, you would have acclimatised yourself when driving or walking up to the building, taking mental notes of how you feel about the following: the entrance, the foyer or reception, colours, scent, and sounds. You do this automatically but often forget about your senses – sight, hearing, smell, taste and touch – which help you determine the probable outcome of any quest. Most of the time you are unaware you are taking this sensory information on board. You might have said to yourself "I cannot explain why, but something didn't feel right."

Using your empowerment tools, and taking the time to get to know how you tick, you will come to learn that your self-awareness is not about one thing but many. These will determine your next move. No matter how much you might want that job if it does not feel right you will turn it down, you will turn away. There are no outside influences here as it is all about you listening to what your

Professional Self, your subconscious mind and your intuitive side is telling you. It feels so good, so empowering when you reach a decision long before you share it with others. It is also a fantastic observational process. If you do share your decision with others, sit back and listen to what they have to say and remember observation. Some might congratulate you while others will run to their personal draw of negativity. Remember to take on board how you react to any external negativity.

Society teaches us that our survival is linked to being accepted, being liked, to belonging. Not so for the person practising their Professional Self, as their first day might go something like this: their first priority is acclimatising to the new job, while getting to know new colleagues is secondary. You understand that giving too much information about your personal life is an open invitation for work colleagues to make assumptions even though they don't know you. Those assumptions might be positive or negative, but why would you put yourself in that situation in the first place? Friendships form naturally over time; rushing in to form an attachment usually ends up sending the wrong signals. Once you return home, talking with family or friends about your day, you would be focused on the job and the challenges it might present and whether you feel comfortable meeting those challenges. There might be a brief mention of colleagues. You then relax with a glass of wine. A good night's sleep follows because yes, you are in control, and if you feel the job is not for you then look for another. Life really does not need to be difficult.

Your new job practising a Personal Self approach might go something like this: you are on major alert; you might experience palpitations, and light headedness in your eagerness to connect and make a good impression. Your aim is to prove your suitability for the new job. While remembering to smile, you might throw in a few self-deprecating comments, a subconscious way of proving you are not a threat. By the end of the day your cheeks ache due to the amount of smiling you have done.

Does this sound like the proverbial hare caught in the headlights?

Once you are home, talking to family, and friends, you will probably concentrate more on the colleagues you met, signalling particular colleagues you feel you connected with. This makes you feel safe. You might go on to describe your workstation, ambiance, where you ate lunch and what you ate. You might have downed a couple of glasses of wine and possibly a couple of headache tablets. Your sleep might be interrupted by a whirl of thoughts about the day, allowing doubts and concerns to add to your tossing and turning. You are probably unaware that you have prioritised fitting in and acceptance by your new colleagues as your main priority. This approach is not so different to a child's first day at school. Therefore, it is a learnt behaviour pattern.

The problem which invariably arises from the need to fit in is being caught up in everyone's business, either from a saving perspective or from a need to belong, and giving too much information to a group of strangers you know nothing about. Still worse, over time this brings with it a lot of personal insecurities. There could be a greater price to pay if you choose to work in Personal Self mode. Promotions may often be hindered, not because of your work, but by colleagues you have allowed to have an effect on you. It is also worth reminding yourself which personality type you originally chose and if this fits with this scenario. Try taking yourself back to an interview you have had in the past and see how much you missed, by the way your subconscious took all the above on board. How much were you listening?

Empowerment Tool 34: *Do I give people too much information about myself*?

Another common example of roles we play is when meeting friends. Think about your friends individually, what they want from you and what you want from them. There is always some need involved here. Some are listeners – what does this say about you? Some enjoy drama in their life – what does it say about them, and what role do you play? Perhaps you depend upon some for advice, perhaps because you admire them? You would like to *be* like them. Ask yourself what personality type you are playing here.

Some friends have a habit of only calling you when they are feeling negative. I wonder why you tolerate this. Do you feel guilty if you do not help them? Remember, guilt is a form of bullying, bending your will. Once more I ask, what role do you think you are playing? More importantly, why are you playing this role in the first instance?

Some friends make you feel ill at ease. You think they are better looking than you are, or more intelligent than you. They belittle you and call it joking. Meanwhile, you convince yourself you are too sensitive. They make snide comments and you can never think of a comeback until later.

But you are prepared to overlook all the above because having friends is more important and more socially acceptable than carrying the label 'billy no mates'. Right? Society really does apply pressure evaluating us on our worth, which includes taking into account how many friends we do or don't have. You are subconsciously aware of your position in the group and the roles you play.

Transferring these feelings to the conscious level of your mind is always the tricky part, because if you are not aware then how can you change? You need to figure out which personality type you are in any setting, because they will change, as will the roles you play. Whether or not you want to continue, these roles can be detrimental. On reflection, if you feel your role with a particular group of friends is detrimental it makes you feel worthless; you become agitated prior to meeting these friends and conscious of how you look and speak. What part of the get together do you actually enjoy? Or is it only when you have downed your fifth shot, in other words when you are past caring, that you enjoy the gathering at all?

These situations really do have an effect on how we see ourselves in society and have consistently arisen in the therapy room over the years across all ages and genders.

Empowerment Tool 35: *How do I feel about my friends*?

Empowerment Tool 36*: How do my friends see me*?

Another role frequently played is that of the chameleon. We almost change our physique when we need to fit in by mirroring the person we are attempting to impress. This certainly applies during interviews. The Chameleon is one of the most basic rules of attraction, fitting in, looking for acceptance and is employed by all ages. It is a manipulation done largely subconsciously. It feeds the observer's ego as they feel they have discovered their other, more appropriate 'self'.

Take a good hard look at your friends. You may not have lots of them, maybe just one. However, perhaps you have chosen this person as a friend in the true sense of the word. You enjoy their company with nothing to prove on either side, but the chances are this friend or friends are equally living their lives from an empowered standpoint. This is the law of attraction at its most positive.

Imagine meeting a friend or friends. They do not judge you as they are not interested how you dress, what your nails look like, what shoes you are wearing, how entertaining you are, or your knowledge on a certain topic. You are completely and unequivocally comfortable with just being you, as they feel exactly the same about themselves. This will automatically bring a positive energy wherever you go and you will feel wonderfully confident because you no longer need to play any role. You have not spent hundreds of pounds having your hair or nails done, a pedicure, new outfit, or downed a couple of shots in an attempt to calm your nerves. It sounds laughable but guess what? This is precisely what many people are doing each time they say yes to an evening spent with friends, and this situation crops up consistently in the therapy room.

Once you really understand who you are, never fear; you will still have those faults, making blunders, losing your temper, saying the wrong thing. The difference is you now have empowerment tools which enable you to stand back and reflect on what went wrong, how you reacted. So you can now rectify the situation. You can choose which role you will play in future or present work. You will refuse to 'carry crap'; this was a client's wonderful description upon realising how much they carried around which was not theirs.

Empowerment Tool 37: *How much crap do I carry which is not mine?*

It serves no purpose other than dragging you down, and making you feel worthless and useless. There is a high probability that it does not even belong to you so yes, you guessed it, give it back and move on with your life.

Summary of Empowerment Tools in this Chapter

31) *Am I the same person when I interact with people compared to the person I am when alone?*

32) *To just be me, no matter where I am. (I don't have to be somebody different in order to be important. I am important to me in my own right and that is all that matters. How I feel about me.)*

33) *During an interview, what role am I playing?*

34) *Do I give people too much information about myself?*

35) *How do I feel about my friends?*

36) How do my friends see me?

37) How much crap do I carry which is not mine?

CHAPTER 8: RELATIONSHIPS

As you move towards self-acceptance and begin to feel good about yourself, I would like to expand your world just for a moment and take a look at romantic relationships in a little more detail.

I hope you have a better understanding now that everyone has their worldview. You have a right to your opinion just as they have a right to theirs. For example, you meet someone and discover you have things in common. First, tick in the box. It is still early days and to an extent you are both on your best behaviour. Communication is the key factor when getting to know each other. Clients often reminisce about earlier times in their relationships, and the hours spent just talking.

Chances are you will be preoccupied with the role you play, fitting in to please; perhaps the chameleon, feeding the significant other's ego. There is often desperation involved when seeking a partner. If you choose the wrong partners repeatedly, the desperation to find the right partner increases.

Perhaps it is time to stop and re-evaluate your thinking. Consider why you feel you need someone in your life in the first place, and what need they can fulfil; a need you cannot fulfil yourself. Whoever you meet, they come with baggage, just as you do. If you feel insecure, lack self-confidence or self-worth, do you think you are capable of handling someone else's issues?

Invariably, a relationship will break down because it is not equal, not 50/50. Often, one partner carries a higher percentage of the relationship. Over time, this situation presents as a burden and this inevitably creates strain.

Opposites do attract. For example, when one partner plays the role of the victim, the other will attempt to be supportive. However, their own needs are not being met and depression is a regular occurrence in such relationships because the balance is not right. Equally, when a partner is dominant or over critical, the partner on the receiving end begins to feel helpless. Their self-esteem is gradually wrecked as they feel they can never please their partner. This becomes their goal, to please, but what happens to them along the way?

Mental and emotional shackling is not conducive to an equal relationship. Think about your personality type. Think also about your childhood influences and ask yourself if you are a person who seeks to please, or are more inclined to look to control or to be controlled. Ask yourself how you see yourself in your relationships, past and present. I wonder why, regardless of behaviour, everything seems to be healed instantly with just three words, namely, "I love you". Try asking yourself why.

Empowerment Tool 38: *What is my definition of love?*

Evaluate your relationship in terms of percentages.

Empowerment Tool 39: *Is my relationship 50/50?*

Whenever I ask my clients this it tends to stop them in their tracks. They take stock of not just the relationship they are in, but their relationships in general.

The one single greatest mistake we as a society have made is to have lost the art of communication. Communicating not only our needs, but feeling strong enough, and being sufficiently aware of ourselves, to listen to what another has to say without trying to save them or dismiss their needs as irrelevant.

Empowerment Tool 40: *What is it that prevents me from telling my significant other exactly how I am feeling?*

Whether you are feeling sad, angry, depressed, dissatisfied or just fed up, perhaps you are afraid to speak openly, afraid of the response, feel they will not be interested, feel they will not understand, afraid they will say "if only you did as I said you would not have this problem" (their worldview) or "If you are not happy you can leave" (dominant) or fear of burdening them as you feel they would not be able to cope (your presumption). If so, then communication has broken down. Equally, how prepared are you to listen to what your 'significant other' has to say?

There are many levels of communication. For example, "How was your day." That is, the running-of-the-house type conversation. Or there is the slightly more serious conversation that involves decision-making. Then the deeper, often more complex conversation that involves feelings. I presume you are okay talking about the day-to-day running of the house. If you feel strongly about making a decision or discussing your feelings in some depth but feel hesitant, it might be a good idea to take a walk, or find a quiet space, and have a long think.

You know this person and their likely reaction. You need to weigh up the pros and cons of having this conversation, what you want to gain from it. Be clear about what you want to communicate, this is your 50 percent. Don't make the error of presuming another's reaction. If you become preoccupied with what your significant other might say or how they might react, then the relationship is not 50/50 and perhaps it is worthwhile asking if you conduct yourself in this way with all relationships, both personal and professional.

Just imagine the millions of people whose relationships, owing to avoidance, each one living in automatic mode, insular within a relationship, are not equal. Avoidance becomes the norm. It has become a 'look the other way' philosophy.

Or maybe they have resigned themselves to believing the situation will never change. There is often the home, finances, and children to consider, and avoidance can lead to drinking, drugs, affairs, and spending increasing time with friends. Now factor in stress, unhappiness, guilt, despair, and depression; all because of fear of the unknown along with avoidance and lack of communication.

Many of us dislike change. This dislike keeps us in jobs and relationships we grow to hate, so we put ourselves through abject misery, which often lasts years. Because we are living in denial, the anger, which can turn to hatred, burns deep. The significant other is often oblivious to this until it is too late to save the relationship. Lack of communication, denial and avoidance are detrimental to you, and the longer you allow them to continue, the deeper emotions such as worthlessness, lack of self-confidence, and detrimental behaviours, which may include starving yourself, or comfort eating, get a foothold.

The only requirement here is that you are honest to yourself – this is your life and with the right partner it could be so good.

Empowerment Tool 41: *If you find it difficult to communicate ask yourself why.*

Sometimes you do need to walk away and change your life. This is not always for the better in material terms, but it is done for your mental wellbeing and you owe it to yourself to be happy. So face those fears, be clear what you want, and begin a new chapter by using clear communication. Your life will flow naturally through phases; careers, life changing events, financial difficulties, illness, deaths. Maintaining a relationship requires commitment and a lot of hard work. Communication will make or break a relationship, so what if it fails? What do you think the cause or causes were and for how long have you been living a lie?

Summary of Empowerment Tools in this Chapter

38) *What is my definition of love?*

39) *Is my relationship 50/50?*

40) *What is it that stops me from telling my significant other exactly how I am feeling?*

41) *If you find it difficult to communicate ask yourself why.*

CHAPTER 9: RECAP

My intention in writing this book was to offer a brief introduction to the main elements of empowerment. Too much information can be counterproductive. You will not become empowered instantly from reading *The 49 Empowerment Tools*, but watch this space. As seeds have been planted you need to allow the tools time to grow.

A brief synopsis of what we have covered so far

Survival is essential to our being in any context. You will do virtually anything to survive.

Identity, self-observation, and *Who am I*? Hopefully, this has got you thinking and in the passing days, weeks and months, conversations – current or past – will resurface. You will begin the challenge of asking yourself "Who am I?"

Group identity and personality types. I hope by now you have a sense of the various roles you subconsciously play in your private and professional life. Many clients have found this particular exercise enlightening and refer to personality types and roles. As they amalgamate their life effectively they begin to self-analyse, take control, and own their life, which automatically leads to feeling empowered.

Learnt behaviour patterns, childhood, mimicking, observation, guilt, passive, and dominant characteristics. I hope you obtained a real sense of your origins, how these first markers in your life have influenced the choices and decisions you have made. I also hope you can go forward with a better understanding and not get bogged down with useless time and energy-wasting feelings of anger and resentment. Negative thoughts really lead nowhere and keep you locked away unable to move forward. If negative thoughts should arise, put them into perspective and remember, ninety percent was not yours to begin with, so why hold on to this negativity all these years later?

Risk and negative thinking: Remember the cauldron; we are more inclined to go down the negative route, i.e. negative thinking. So be aware of the familiar and prepare to face challenges. Seek out the unfamiliar, this is all about you.

Roles we play: Once again, defining who we feel we need to be within society's rules. This is nothing to do with us as individuals. By removing personality types, learnt behaviour, guilt – there is no place here for passive or dominant characteristics – roles become irrelevant. The role you play is always yourself whether at work or home, professionally or privately. The Professional Self is alert to the fact there is a job to be done and much to learn. You have committed yourself, which, remember, you chose to do. The Private Self can take in everything else which is not work-related. You can clearly define your roles whilst remaining true to yourself. When you leave work you also leave your professional mindset behind; please remember that you are always in control – only ever do what you want to do.

You are not perfect and so there is little point pretending to be. Don't be afraid to ask yourself pertinent questions; challenge yourself, question those doubts and uncertainties when you need to. Above all else, listen to what you have to say.

Relationships and evaluating equality is relatively easily done by stepping back and observing your relationships – not only with your significant other but equally within all forms of interaction. Communication is a problem not only for the individual but also within society; we rarely ask ourselves of what we are afraid.

Lack of communication is detrimental to you and you owe it to yourself to be honest about how you feel, what you think matters only to you. Once you understand what makes you tick then managing your life will seem effortless because you always come first in your decision making. You already know reading this there are difficult conversations ahead of you; what you need to understand and be ready for is that there will be changes and we do not as a society like change. This is why you should prepare yourself for what you want. Be very clear in your mind and be focused on what you want the outcome to be. Equality and empowerment go hand in hand so always look for that 50/50 in all your relationships, whether personal or professional. Treat others how you would like to be treated but do not be disillusioned when people do not accommodate you; you are still learning and will continue to make mistakes until you have built the personal portfolio of your life. When you are in your good place, other people's moods, angry words, reactions, indifference, etc. may hurt but you have the tools to step back, reflect, and deflect that hurt to your periphery. All this negativity is not yours, so why hang onto it?

You possess intuition, but often due to your being indoctrinated into believing that others have all the answers, which encompasses what you read, hear, watch and observe, it is overlooked. In effect, you need to think about influences in your life. I wonder what your reaction would be if I were to say the following:

Empowerment Tool 42: *All intuition requires is listening to and trusting yourself.*

Under the umbrella of society, we feel safe; we normalise our behaviour based on our external observations. Advertising and credit on tap, etc., all feed into the 'want more' society, but the more we want, the more we become indebted to the 'keeping up with the Jones's' lifestyle. We become increasingly detached from choices and individuality because ultimately we are looking for acceptance from others. Where have the dreams and goals gone? Where has risk gone? We receive a daily dose of negativity; which feeds fear of failure.

You may recall I spoke of childhood, acceptance, and failure? Even though we cannot always verbalise what that elusive failure is, fear and doubt drive us to close ranks, and this often begins with closing our minds.

For some odd reason, when I introduce the idea of intuition knee-jerk reaction leads invariably to a question "Is that spiritual?" There appears to be a fear involved when thinking and listening independently. Intuition encompasses the interaction of your five senses. Animal survival is dependent on the use of their senses but I do not recall reading about an animal being described as spiritual.

Do you see how the indoctrination of fear and doubt inhibits us from autonomy? Think back to one of the perhaps many times in your life when you just had a feeling about something, a gut feeling. Perhaps the feeling was clear, perhaps a little hazy. If you acted on that feeling and diverted your course of action, then that was your intuition guiding you. The point being that you listened and acted on that feeling. This is listening to your intuition.

Unfortunately, society does not accept intuition; society encourages logic, objective thinking. It chooses a scientific outcome and visual stimulation when determining the next course of action. Intuition or gut feeling is gaining ground. We are beginning to ask questions, though fear of the unknown versus tangible evidence remains a dividing point. Intuition is not a question for society to answer. It is a personal quest, a personal growth, it is about *you*.

A client explained their interpretation of intuition, or, as they called it, a gut feeling. "I think it is learning to trust yourself about decision making. Trust what you are thinking. It is a deep trust, it is to listen where you are going and not to be influenced with what others are saying."

A way of exploring your intuition is to sit quietly for a few minutes and listen to what you have to say. Listen to your fears. Imagine yourself in a situation you would like an answer to. To yourself. Close your eyes if it helps and just listen. Let the usual fears, doubts and uncertainty wash over you. This is your automatic protective mode. It will tell you not to do something, but when challenged it has no answer – it's a feeling and no more than that. Let that feeling emerge, go deeper, pick up what you are sensing. Don't push it, give yourself time and gradually you will notice how your thoughts and senses intertwine.

Empowerment Tool 43: *Trust your intuition. It will grow as your confidence in yourself grows.*

By now I hope you have a clearer view of who you are and where you identify yourself within society. More importantly, how you tick, how you are beginning to enjoy yourself as you test unchartered waters and perhaps find your confidence is beginning to grow. I hope you can see with greater clarity that you do matter, your opinions are relevant, and if others attempt to subdue you this really has nothing to do with you but says an awful lot about them. Observation of yourself and others only brings greater clarity and confirmation of your individual identity.

The next time you have a feeling, about an object perhaps, or a person, just concentrate on it for a while, watch the outcome and build your awareness. Imagine the day when you do not need to feed your stress, sadness or loneliness with materialism. Imagine letting your natural intuitive side in, then ask yourself a question: sit back and wait for the answer. That is all it takes.

Summary of Empowerment Tools in this Chapter

> 42) *All intuition requires is listening to yourself and trusting yourself.*

> 43) *Trust your intuition. It will grow as your confidence in yourself grows.*

CHAPTER 11: SELF CONCEPT

You have reached the final chapter in *The 49 Empowerment Tools*. Hopefully, you have absorbed and possibly re-read parts of this book, put it down, had a long think and questioned yourself on many aspects. For instance, how you have lived your life up until today and how you respond to others.

Now it is time to take a look at self-concept.

Self-concept is the cherry on top of the cake. Empowerment really begins to take shape when you understand self-concept, which involves every part of you. This is what you have been building over the past 10 chapters. Self-concept represents your belief system, where you see yourself in society, your appearance, and your interpretation of how others see you.

Empowerment Tool 44: *I am my best friend and no one knows me as well as I know me.*

Empowerment Tool 45: *I will never let myself down.*

Empowerment Tool 46: *I have complete trust in the choices I make in my life. This is about me, no one else.*

Self-concept incorporates knowledge and your attitudes, whether negative or positive. I usually introduce self-concept to clients by inviting them to explain how they would describe themselves from a third-person perspective. For example, I invite K to explain to me who they think (and feel) K is. This exercise might seem a little strange to begin with, but persevere as the rewards are quite significant once you begin to view yourself 'outside of the box'. You can do this exercise sitting quietly and just listening to what you have to say about yourself. If you have read this book to the final chapter you should be confident about addressing quite a few areas of your life. Give yourself time to think about your self-concept. The natural step forward from self-concept is proactive thinking.

Tool forty-seven: *No one else has the power to make me happy. My life is mine and I need to own it.*

Proactive thinking is all about accepting who you are, but equally accepting where you are in your life. Proactive thinking is considering situations as they arise and not reacting before you have had time to assess the situation. This is the key. This mindset lends you the confidence not to be dragged into making hasty decisions. You are in control, you need time to think, take a step back, and to let the intuitive side of you in. You need to weigh up the pros and cons and figure out what is the best course of action for you.

The more you practise this tool, proactive thinking, the more confident you will become, and assertiveness will naturally accompany the new proactive you.

There is never a need to be the loudest, the cleverest, the wittiest in the room, as these things are usually a mask to cover neediness and lack of self-confidence.

I often wonder why people feel threatened by a confident person? How can anyone take a dislike to someone they barely know – or has this person evoked a feeling or a memory that lay unresolved? If you feel threatened by a confident person, then this is yours to sort out.

In any situation take time to think about what you want, what suits you, what will make you happy. Imagine the final outcome and how you want a situation to go. Never allow yourself to feel under pressure. This is yours, so own it. Once you have accepted who you are, taken time to get to know you, listened to what your intuition has to say, and taken a proactive stance, maybe then it is time to realise your potential.

Potential is one of my personal favourites of the empowerment tools. Hopefully, you have navigated through the many corridors of your subconscious. Perhaps you started your journey and gingerly opened doors. Maybe this process has gained momentum as your confidence has grown. Finally, you reach the end of the corridor seeing that in front of you is the largest door. It can be any colour you choose; written on the door in bold letters is *potential*.

Empowerment Tool 48: *A Proactive Self is to be the best I can, to have passion about whatever I do, to have confidence in myself and to have complete trust in myself.*

Empowerment Tool 49: *I have the potential to succeed. It is already there so all I need to do is to reach in and take it.*

It takes courage to step through this door as there might be challenges, self-doubts that creep in, and that little voice that whispers, "Don't rock the boat, stay where you are, it's safe." The problem with this thinking is that if you choose to stay put, this is as good as your life is going to get. So take a long think about where you are today: what is missing from your life, what you want from your life, what your dreams are. Now start making goals, small ones to begin with. Test out this new territory. Remember to congratulate yourself on a daily basis. No matter what achievement you have made that day, it is your achievement, so own it. As you open your mind, so your potential will begin to grow.

These are examples of some clients who discovered their potential:

Client A: An aisle personality: keeping others happy was their goal in life. This led to depression, a sense of hopelessness, and no hope for their future. Today, friendships are no longer a priority, pleasing people even less so. Self-drive, self-belief, setting personal goals and looking forward to a fantastic future is a proactive reality.

Client B: A front middle personality, lost in the various roles played, too many goals, working 24/7, addicted to the adrenaline rush of how fast or for how long they could keep going.

Today client B is proactive in making personal happiness and changes a priority. They have discovered awareness.

Client C: A middle personality, keen to be a part of a group resulting in loss of self-identity.

Today C acknowledges they are a part of each group, but is equally mindful of their identity, and they are considering a career change.

Client D: A shepherd/shepherdess keen to save, keen to remain obscure, only stepping up to the mark for a cause not associated with themselves.

Today client D has discovered the power of their worldview, what they think and feel does matter to them. Client D speaks with increasing confidence and no longer fears reprisal or criticism. Client D recently stated: "It is not mine but theirs."

Summary of Empowerment Tools in this Chapter

44) *I am my best friend, no one knows me as well as I know me.*

45) *I will never let myself down.*

46) I have complete trust in the choices I make in my life. This is about me, no one else.

47) No one else has the power to make me happy. My life is mine and I need to own it.

48) A Proactive Self is to be the best I can, to have passion about whatever I do, to have confidence in myself and to have complete trust in myself.

49) I have the potential to succeed, it is already there, all I need to do is to reach in and take it.

AFTERWORD

I hope this first volume of *Empowerment Tools* series has assisted you in building your personal platform. You have forty-nine tools to work with, and you will need to be repetitive in going over these tools many times because we naturally resist change. This leads to the unknown, which is sufficient reason for many to turn back. Persistence and determination to change your life is the key, so give yourself time to adjust, time to learn, time to trust your instincts, time to sit back and to observe and time to challenge yourself when faced with life challenges.

Clients discover they often go backwards to begin with until they see changes happening, which gives them the confidence to move forward. This see-saw effect will persist for some time, so don't lose heart as you will eventually begin to change your mindset, and start thinking and acting independently.

In my second book of Empowerment Tools, I will be exploring anxiety, depression, panic, victim mode, and much more. I look forward to the continuation of our work.

ACKNOWLEDGEMENTS

I decided to begin writing about my experiences through my work with clients over the years. This book would not have been possible without them and for this I thank them all.

I would like to thank my husband who gave his time and experience in helping me collate this book. I would like to thank my family who have given me invaluable support.

I have corresponded over the years with Angela Donovan – a world-renowned medium, spiritualist and business mentor. Angela not only offered a great deal of practical business sense, she also guided me in my approach to writing this first book, her support and belief in this project has been unwavering and I would like to take the opportunity to thank her.

I also would like to thank Angela Carter, a loyal colleague who has offered sound advice. Also Laurence Jones, my proof-reader thank you.

Thank you to Gary Dalkin my Editor, his invaluable help, advice and professionalism has surpassed my expectations.

Finally, a big thank you to **BeDot Media Group** and the unwavering support on the book design and my website to accompany the book: **www.thefortyninetools.com**

Printed in Great Britain
by Amazon